A Writer's Notebook

JAMES HAZELL

You can't wait for inspiration.
You have to go after it with a club.

—JACK LONDON (1876–1916)
American writer and novelist

Writing is the only thing that, when I do it, I don't feel I should be doing something else.

—GLORIA STEINEM, b. 1934
American writer

DAN BURNE
JONES·B·A·E·

Read, read, read. Read everything—trash, classics, good and bad, and see how they do it. Just like a carpenter who works as an apprentice and studies the mast. Read! You'll absorb it. Then write. If it is good, you'll find out. If it's not, throw it out the window.

—WILLIAM FAULKNER (1897–1962)
American novelist

Always grab the reader by the throat in the first paragraph, sink your thumbs into his windpipe in the second, and hold him against the wall until the tag line.

—PAUL O'NEIL, Twentieth century
American writer

There are very few writers who are not cranks in some way.

—PAUL THEROUX, b. 1941
American writer and novelist

EX LIBRIS

CHARLES HOLME

W hen I went to school, I knew poetry was not a dead thing. I knew it was always written by the living, even though the dateline said the man was dead.

—STEPHEN VINCENT BENÉT (1898–1943)
American poet and storywriter

Too many poets delude themselves by thinking the mind is dangerous and must be left out. Well, the mind is dangerous and must be left in.

—ROBERT FROST (1874–1963)
American poet

The history of the American novel has been one of writers thinking they had nothing to write about and then discovering they did.

—LE ANNE SCHREIBER, b. 1945
American writer

A. GERTRVDE ORCHARD

AS THE SVN COLOVRS
FLOWERS SO ART
COLOVRS LIFE.

A *good rule for writers: Do not explain overmuch.*

—W[illiam] SOMERSET MAUGHAM (1874–1965)
English novelist and playwright

I never know quite when a book starts. I don't worry about it too much. I don't believe in forcing the pace. I take it when I can, sort of seize the moment.

—HELEN MacINNES, b. 1907
American novelist

I wrote about old people long before I was anything like as old as that, because I didn't know about them. I still write out of an enormous sense of curiosity. As I get older, I write more about children, because I've forgotten what it's like to be a child.

—WILLIAM TREVOR COX, b. 1928
Irish-born English novelist, playwright, and storywriter

F*acts and truth really don't have much to do with each other.*

—WILLIAM FAULKNER (1897–1962)
American novelist

The writer should never be ashamed of staring. There is nothing that does not require his attention.

—FLANNERY O'CONNOR (1925–1964)
American novelist and storywriter

W hat I adore is supreme professionalism. I'm bored by writers who can write only when it is raining.

—NOEL COWARD (1899–1973)
English playwright and songwriter

ex libris:
HANS MILLY WITT

I cannot write more than three or four lines of longhand without fainting. Even if I could, I wouldn't be able to compose on anything but a typewriter, probably a bad habit from newspaper days.

—ROBERT BENCHLEY (1889–1945)
American humorist

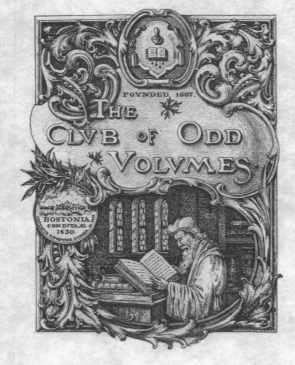

When I'm writing a novel, I'm dealing with a double life. I live in the present at the same time that I live in the past with my characters. It is this that makes a novelist so eccentric and unpleasant.

—J[ohn] P[hillips] MARQUAND (1893–1960)
American novelist

*O*ne ought to write only when one leaves a piece of one's flesh in the inkpot each time one dips one's pen.

—COUNT LEO NIKOLAYEVICH TOLSTOY (1828–1910)
Russian novelist and philosopher

A work that aspires, however humbly, to the condition of art should carry its justification in every line.

—JOSEPH CONRAD (1857–1924)
Ukranian-born English writer

I *think a little menace is fine to have in a story. For one thing, it's good for the circulation.*

—RAYMOND CARVER. b. 1938
American writer

I began to write short pieces when I was living
in a room too small to write a novel in.

—ANGELA CARTWRIGHT, Twentieth century
American writer

In the two or three or four months that it takes me to write a play, I find that the reality of the play is a great deal more alive for me than what passes for reality.

—EDWARD ALBEE, b. 1928
American playwright

I like density, not volume. I like to leave something to the imagination. The reader must fit the pieces together, with the author's discreet help.

—MAUREEN HOWARD, b. 1930
American writer

Everywhere I go, I'm asked if I think the universities stifle writers. My opinion is that they don't stifle enough of them.

—FLANNERY O'CONNOR (1925–1964)
American novelist and storywriter

Not all writers are artists. But all of us like the idea of somebody in the year 2283 blowing the dust off one of our books, thumbing through it and exclaiming, "Hey, listen to what this old guy had to say back in the twentieth century!"

—WILLIAM ATTWOOD, b. 1919
American writer, ambassador, and former publisher of Newsday

SAPIENTIA
NON MORTIS
SED VITAE
MEDITATIO EST

B·V·A·ROLING

A *novel is an impression, not an argument.*

—THOMAS HARDY (1840–1928)
English poet and novelist

Like many journalists, I am often frustrated that my insights have, at most, a one-day shelf life, and I yearn for the relative immortality of good paper and hard covers.

—THOMAS HINE, b. 1947
American newspaperman

I think it can be dangerous for young writers to be modest when they're young. I've known a number of truly talented writers who did less than they could have done because they weren't vain and unpleasant enough about their talent. You have to take it seriously.

—NORMAN MAILER, b. 1923
American novelist and writer

The art of writing is the art of applying the seat of the pants to the seat of the chair.

—MARY HEATON VORSE (1881–1966)
American writer

VITA SINE LIBRIS
FLORENCE CAMPBELL
MORS EST

I am breaking my heart over this story,
and cannot bear to finish it.

—CHARLES DICKENS (1812–1870)
English novelist and storywriter

In my own experience, nothing is harder for the developing writer than overcoming his anxiety that he is fooling himself and cheating or embarrassing his family and friends. To most people, even those who don't read much, there is something special and vaguely magical about writing, and it is not easy for them to believe that someone they know—someone quite ordinary in many respects—can really do it.

—JOHN GARDNER (1912–1982)
American novelist and writer

I'm a Hollywood writer, so I put on a sports jacket and take off my brain.

—BEN HECHT (1894–1964)
American screenwriter, playwright, and storywriter

*S*ince great writers communicate a vision of existence, one can't usually borrow their methods. The method is married to the vision.

—NORMAN MAILER, b. 1923
American novelist and writer

FROM THE
COOK BOOKS OF
CLEM HALL

There is no point asserting and reasserting
what the heart cannot believe.

—ALEKSANDER ISAYEVICH SOLZHENITSYN, b. 1918
Russian novelist

If you cannot conveniently tumble out of a balloon, or be swallowed up in an earthquake, or get stuck fast in a chimney, you will have to be contented with simply imagining some similar misadventure.

—EDGAR ALLAN POE (1809–1849)
American poet, critic, and storywriter

Many writers have preconceived ideas about what literature is supposed to be, and their ideas seem to exclude that which makes them most charming in private conversation.

—ALLEN GINSBERG, b. 1926
American poet

I rather fancy most authors think of a character and then think of what he would do, while I think of something to be done and then think of the most interesting character to do it.

—C[ecil] S[cott] FORESTER (1899–1966)
English-born American novelist

I *go with Robert Louis Stevenson, who said that an intelligent reader with imagination can make an ``Iliad'' out of a newspaper.*

—CARL SANDBURG (1878–1967)
American poet and biographer

I *see only one rule: to be clear. If I am not clear,*
then my entire world crumbles into nothing.

—STENDHAL (Marie Henri Beyle. 1783–1842)
French novelist

The deepest quality of a work of art will always be the quality of the mind of the producer. . . . No good novel will ever proceed from a superficial mind.

—HENRY JAMES (1843–1916)
American-born English writer

Try this: Carefully memorize the meaning of a passage, then read it;
you'll find you can actually read it without the words' making any sound whatever
in the mind's ear.

—WILLIAM BURROUGHS, b. 1914
American novelist

In times of unrest and fear, it is perhaps the writer's duty to celebrate, to single out some of the values we can cherish, to talk about some of the few warm things we know in a cold world.

—PHYLLIS McGINLEY, b. 1905
American poet

I had been a humor writer all my life, but when I was writing this novel, I said,
"Ah ha, because this is important, it can't be funny." A great fallacy!

—JUDITH MARTIN, b. 1938
American columnist and writer

If you told me to write a love song tonight, I'd have a lot of trouble. But if you tell me to write a love song about a girl with a red dress who goes into a bar and is on her fifth martini and is falling off her chair, that's a lot easier, and it makes me free to say anything I want.

—STEPHEN SONDHEIM, b. 1930
American lyricist and songwriter

Our words must seem to be inevitable.

—WILLIAM BUTLER YEATS (1865–1939)
Irish poet and dramatist

Never save anything for your next book, because that possible creation may not be properly shaped to hold the thoughts you're working with today. In fiction especially, anything that could happen, should happen.

—TAM MOSSMAN, b. 1945
American editor, writer, and art critic

I don't make myself work. It's just the thing I want to do. To be completely alone in a room, to know that there'll be no interruptions and I've got eight hours is exactly what I want—yeah, just paradise.

—WILLIAM BURROUGHS, b. 1914
American novelist

It is fatal for anyone who writes to think of their sex. It is fatal to be a man or woman pure and simple; one must be woman-manly or man-womanly.

—VIRGINIA WOOLF (1882–1941)
English novelist and diarist

I think that one's art is a growth inside one. I do not think one can explain growth. It is silent and subtle. One does not keep digging up a plant to see how it grows.

—EMILY CARR (1871—1945)
Canadian artist and writer

Ideas come very easily with you, incessantly, like a stream. With me, it is a tiny thread of water. Hard labor at art is necessary for me before obtaining a waterfall.

—GUSTAVE FLAUBERT (1821–1880)
French novelist

By reading what he has last written, just before he recommences his task, the writer will catch the tone and spirit of what he is then saying, and will avoid the fault of seeming to be unlike himself.

—ANTHONY TROLLOPE (1815–1882)
English novelist

To write simply is as difficult as to be good.

—W[illiam] SOMERSET MAUGHAM (1874–1965)
English novelist and playwright

If Picasso displaces an eye to make a portrait jump into life, that is one thing. If I displace a word to restore some of its freshness, that is a far, far more difficult thing.

—JEAN COCTEAU (1889–1963)
French poet, writer, and filmmaker

If you spend eight hours a day thinking about something obsessively, you're bound to be ahead of anyone else. Then once you're ahead, in terms of what you know about the subject, you add a dash of melodrama, and there you are.

—RICHARD CONDON, b. 1915
American novelist

Not everything has a name. Some things lead us into a realm beyond words . . . By means of art we are sometimes sent—dimly, briefly— revelations unattainable by reason.

—ALEKSANDER ISAYEVICH SOLZHENITSYN, b. 1918
Russian novelist

The trade of authorship is a violent and indestructible obsession.

—GEORGE SAND (Amandine Aurore Lucie Dupin. 1804–1876)
French novelist and writer

My proof corrections consist of fights with proofreaders who know more about "Webster's Unabridged" than about life.

—WILLIAM McFEE (1881–1966)
English-born American writer

I have a great responsibility
because I can afford to be honest.

—MAY SARTON, b. 1912
American poet and novelist

Aus den Büchern des Professor
Dr Max kirmis aus fraustadt

The writing itself has been as important to me as the product, and I have always been somewhat indifferent as to whether I have been working on a solemn novel or an impertinent paragraph for "The New Yorker."

—SINCLAIR LEWIS (1885—1951)
American novelist and writer

I write as straight as I can, just as I walk as straight as I can, because that is the best way to get there.

—H[erbert] G[eorge] WELLS (1866–1946)
English novelist and historian

At first they'll reject everything, particularly in your case. What you do is keep sending the same poems to the same people—after a decent interval, of course. After about the fourth or fifth time, they will actually have read them, and they will hear a little bell ring that they'll call the shock of recognition, and they'll take one.

—R[ichard] P[almer] BLACKMUR (1904–1965)
American writer

Nighttime is really the best time to work. All the ideas are there to be yours because everyone else is asleep.

—CATHERINE O'HARA, Twentieth century
American actress

I used to be adjective-happy. Now I cut them with so much severity that I find I have to put a few adjectives back.

The only time I know that something is true is at the moment I discover it in the act of writing.

—JEAN MALAQUAIS, b. 1908
French novelist

Whether we are describing a king, an assassin, a thief, an honest man, a prostitute, a nun, a young girl, or a stallholder in a market, it is always ourselves that we are describing.

—GUY DE MAUPASSANT (1850–1893)
French novelist and storywriter

MARY · B · BUDGETT ·

Writing is so difficult that I often feel that writers, having had their hell on earth, will escape all punishment hereafter.

—JESSAMYN WEST, b. 1907
American writer

The reader, you should premise, will always dislike you and your book. He thinks it an insult that you should dare to claim his attention, and if lunch be announced or there is a ring at the bell, he will welcome the digression. So you will provide him with what he thinks are digressions—with occasions on which he thinks he may let his attention relax . . . But really not one single thread must ever escape your purpose.

—FORD MADOX FORD (1873–1939)
English writer

A novelist's vice usually resembles his virtue, for what he does best he also tends to do to excess.

—JOHN IRVING, b. 1942
American novelist

EX·LIBRIS·
AGNES·J·RUDD·

The·ever·welcome·
company·of·BOOKS·
(Wordsworth)

No iron can pierce the heart with such force
as a period put just at the right place.

—ISAAC BABEL (1894–1941)
Russian storywriter and journalist

W·A·KITTREDGE

What I had to face, the very bitter lesson that everyone who wants to write has got to learn, was that a thing may in itself be the finest piece of writing one has ever done, and yet have absolutely no place in the manuscript one hopes to publish.

—THOMAS WOLFE (1900–1938)
American novelist

EX LIBRIS

NORA ‖‖ BEATRICE ‖‖
DICKSEE

A *good writer sells out everybody*
he knows, sooner or later.

—ALICE McDERMOTT, b. 1953
American writer

*U*nless I know what sort of doorknob his fingers closed on, how shall I—satisfactorily to myself—get my character out of doors?

—FORD MADOX FORD (1873–1939)
English writer

Poetry. I like to think of it as statements
made on the way to the grave.

—DYLAN THOMAS (1914–1953)
Welsh poet

It was unavoidable, my writing. I feel I had no choice in the matter, no more than I had about an unfortunate bone structure and a healthy head of hair.

—MAUREEN HOWARD, b. 1930
American writer

In his work, the artist should be like God in creation: invisible and all-powerful. He should be felt everywhere and seen nowhere.

—GUSTAVE FLAUBERT (1821–1880)
French novelist

The more articulate one is, the more dangerous words become.

—MAY SARTON, b. 1912
American poet and novelist

The most valuable writing habit I have is not to answer questions about my writing habits.

Half my life is an act of revision.

—JOHN IRVING, b. 1942
American novelist

ALTER·CRANE

A Book of Verses underneath the Bough,
A Jug of Wine, a Loaf of Bread—&Thou
Beside me singing in the Wilderness—
Oh, Wilderness were Paradise enow!
: Rubáiyát of Omar Khayyam :

*F*ortunately both my wife and my mother-in-law seem to love digging up mistakes in spelling, punctuation, etc. I can hear them in the next room laughing at me.

—SHERWOOD ANDERSON (1876–1941)
American writer

Centre Panel drawn by C.W. Sherborn, 1911

W hen a successful author analyzes the reasons for his success,
he generally underestimates the talent he was born with, and overestimates his skill
in employing it.

—W[ystan] H[ugh] AUDEN (1907–1973)
English-born American poet

Each author is in every essential a foreigner but lately emigrated from the one land which is comprehensible to him.

—JAMES BRANCH CABELL (1879–1958)
American novelist and essayist

I would feel enormous satisfaction
in being regarded as the voice
of the average American.

—THORNTON WILDER (1897–1975)
American playwright and novelist

1894

GERALDINE
COUNTESS
OF MAYO

The extent of my audience pleases me.
It ranges from Gertrude Stein to stevedores.

—MARY ROBERTS RINEHART (1876–1958)
American novelist

There is also the minority of gifted, willful people who are determined to live their own lives to the end, and writers belong in this class.

—GEORGE ORWELL (Eric Blair, 1903–1950)
English novelist and essayist

NEW YORK YACHT CLUB LIBRARY

NOS AGIMVR TVMIDIS VELIS

Nº

E.D.French sc.   PRESENTED BY   1900

Any work of art, provided it springs from a sincere motivation to further understanding between people, is an act of faith and therefore is an act of love.

—TRUMAN CAPOTE (1924–1984)
American novelist and writer

I'm not sure a bad person can write a good book. If art doesn't make us better, then what on earth is it for?

—ALICE WALKER, b. 1944
American novelist

The manuscript consisted of letter paper, wrapping paper, programs, envelopes, paper napkins—in short, whatever would take the imprint of a pencil. A great deal of it was written with a child crawling around my neck or being sick in my lap, and I dare say this may account for certain aspects of its style.

—AGNES DE MILLE, b. 1906
American dancer and choreographer

If I have to talk about a book that I have written it destroys the pleasure I have from writing it. If the writing is any good everything there is to say has been conveyed to the reader.

—ERNEST HEMINGWAY (1899–1961)
American novelist

To be occasionally quoted
is the only fame I hope for.

—ALEXANDER SMITH (1830–1867)
Scottish writer

W rite without pay until somebody offers pay. If nobody offers pay within three years, the candidate may look upon this circumstance with the most implicit confidence as the sign that sawing wood is what he was intended for.

—MARK TWAIN (Samuel Langhorne Clemens, 1835–1910)
American novelist and humorist

The demonic paradox of writing: when you put something down that happened, people often don't believe it; whereas you can make up anything, and people assume it must have happened to you.

—ANDREW HOLLERAN, b. 1944
American novelist

Writing has made me rich—not in money but in a couple hundred characters out there, whose pursuits and anguish and triumphs I've shared. I am unspeakably grateful at the life I have come to lead.

—WRIGHT MORRIS, b. 1910
American novelist